Loving Norway!
A Kid's Guide To Stavanger, Norway

Photography by John D. Weigand
Poetry by Penelope Dyan

Bellissima Publishing, LLC
Jamul, California
www.bellissimapublishing.com

Copyright © 2017 by Penny D. Weigand and John D. Weigand

All rights reserved. No part of this book may be
reproduced or transmitted in any form or by any means,
electronic or mechanical, including photocopying,
recording, or by any other means, or by any information or
storage retrieval system, without permission from the publisher.

ISBN 978-1-61477-277-4
First Edition

"Great things are done when men and mountains meet."

William Blake

Loving Norway!
Bellissima Publishing, LLC

Introduction

Stavanger is a city in southwestern Norway. A Cathedral in the center of town, Stavanger Cathedral, dates all the way back to the city's 12th-century founding. Stavanger Museum chronicles the city history and displays preserved wildlife. The Norwegian Petroleum Museum displays the oil industry with submersibles, a large drill bit and an escape chute; and the shopping street is well known for its colorful houses! It's also a very interesting place to get to, because you can arrive by car, train or bus; and there's lots to see along the way!

Award winning author, attorney and former teacher, Penelope Dyan, and photographer, John D. Weigand, took an elegant ferry from Bergen, Norway, to Stavanger, that was complete with a restaurant with delicious food! See a bit of what they saw on their trip to this delightful city, as you practice your reading skills using this book filled with word recognition and word repetition and rhyme. This book is the perfect size for a kid's backpack, and its large print is easy on young eyes. Then, when you are done, watch the free music video that goes with this book (on Bellissimavideo's YouTube channel) to see even more of Stavanger, and have even more learning fun!

Loving Norway!
Bellissima Publishing, LLC

Loving Norway!
A Kid's Guide To Stavanger, Norway

Photography by John D. Weigand
Poetry by Penelope Dyan

You hop aboard a ferry.
You're going to Stavanger, Norway
(from Bergen.)
Mom says,
"It isn't really VERY far!"
You shrug your shoulders
(hoping you won't get seasick.)
Because it's more fun than going
by train or bus or car!

After you board the ferry,
you notice a comfortable place to eat.
Forgetting about your queasy tummy,
YOU ask for something sweet.
Then, as excited as Mom
can POSSIBLY be,
she suggests you ALL sit down,
for some cake and some tea!

(You look out the ferry's window.)
First, you see one boat.

And then you see TWO!
Dad says,
"You'll see a lot more boats
than THIS,
before THIS voyage is through!"

Near the Ferry you see
a tall building of red.
It's hoisting up a ship's cargo
right over your head!

You see what looks like fresh onions
all displayed in a pot.
They don't look like many;
but Mom says when they make
soup of them,
of onion soup they'll make a lot.
She says, "Add some peas and carrots,
and a potato or two ,
salt, pepper, garlic and water,
and then let it stew!"
Dad says,
"They look like flower bulbs to me!"
Mom says,
"If we could taste one,
then we'd find out and see!"

You see a cathedral made of stone.
Mom reminds you,
"When you are in God's house,
you are NEVER alone!"

You see an old fashioned looking car.
And THEN you see what
looks like a spaceship
ready to take off for a STAR!
You ask your dad what it is.
He says,
"I really do not know."
You tell him,
"If that's a flying saucer,
I wonder WHERE it will go!"

Mom shakes her head, laughing,
as you walk down the street.
The cobblestones sound hollow,
beneath your two feet.

It's cold, rainy and drippy.
You all open umbrellas over your heads.
Mom suggests its time to go back
to the hotel,
and crawl right into your hotel beds!

You decide to stop
and to have something to eat.
(Mom complains
about HER aching feet.)
When you go into the restaurant,
it is WARM inside,
and from the cold, cold weather,
for awhile you'll hide.

The sky darkens
The night calls out to you.
You are VERY sorry this day is through.
Mom says that SHE is cold.
And Dad complains that HE feels old!
As for you,
you run far, far ahead,
knowing that VERY soon,
you'll be warm and cozy in bed!
And you are happy that tomorrow
is another day,
with another chance
to run and learn,
and to explore and play.

"Do not follow where the path may lead.
Go instead where there is no path and leave a trail."

Ralph Waldo Emerson

www.ingramcontent.com/pod-product-compliance
Ingram Content Group UK Ltd.
Pitfield, Milton Keynes, MK11 3LW, UK
UKHW060134240426

12048UKWH00002B/28